Songs of shoreless winds

By: Nivedita Singh Tomar

Lapsus Creations

First published in India 2020 by Lapsus Creations.
An imprint of Lapsus.

Editing by Anamika Shukla
Book Cover Design by Manish Kumar
Illustrations by Manish Kumar
First Edition May 2020

Published by Lapsus Creations E-mail at
getintouch@lapsuscreations.com
www.lapsuscreations.com

Acknowledgement

I have never thought about a day when I will be holding my own book in my hands. It's such a precious moment of my life that couldn't have been possible without God's grace. Life comes up with myriad of ups and downs. I have been sailing through all these because my parents have bestowed me with great resilience. I am so thankful to them.

I would also like to say thanks to those souls who have made appearance in my life though for temporary moments. They have directly and indirectly taught me a lot.

Sabina Yesmin, this amazing person deserves much more thanks. The confidence and faith of minutest amount that I hold in myself derives its source from her. I hope words keep breathing and enthuse us with life and beauty and good.

About the Author

Our author Nivedita Singh Tomar of the book "Songs of shoreless winds" is just an ordinary girl living a routine simple life. Apart from being an articulate writer she plays low on social skills too, which is why reading and writing dwelled in her life. As far as reading is concerned she isn't a very literary kind of person. She is more involved in reading areas like political science, history and bits of philosophy. At times, the science student in her takes her into utterly objective analysis of the Universe. She mostly finds her poems raw and crude because of her wandered reading habits. Apart from that she likes listening to old bollywood songs which can cheer up her mood any time. As she quotes, she is mostly jumbled up, seeking her own self kind of being. She never plans anything in life. She believes in just moving with the flow and contemplating every morning about what's going to be unfolded for her the particular day.

About the Book

Songs of Shoreless Winds can be defined best as plain flow of the author's heart and obviously her untouched thoughts. At myriad moments whatever things gripped her heart, they did find expression in poems that her pen spilled. Somewhere, it's the author's attempt to be at ease with herself, to find peace. Somewhere, it's a misadventure on her part to cross into the territory of love. She mostly have tried to seek life through each and every word of her poems. There is a meaning to life. May be, the author feels that she is going to spend her whole life in search of that meaning. "Songs of Shoreless Winds" is an ardent effort in that exact direction. Will winds be able to be harboured at correct shore or not? This isn't the real question at all. Reality is the journey undertaken by winds in their quest. This journey is making the author up bit by bit.

HIM

His eyes used to glimmer with smiles,
In between the pauses his words took
In a very secretive manner.
His conversations became
Inseparable constituent of my life's book.

Phrases he commonly brought to apply
Have been etched on my memory's slate.
Intermittent silences born
Out of his hesitance,
Though had much more
To convey, to relate.

In the space of tiny pauses he produced,
I had crafted an entire world to live.
Imaginary but my soul
Breathed there in real,
To an exquisite solace

I was effortlessly adhered.

His unspoken love I had
There to imbibe in,
Nurturing some divine calm within.
All seasons were replete
With utter love under that sky.
Though feet on ground
I felt unchained vibes of flying.

I was falling for a dream
In thorough neglect of reality.
Dream was unuttered but true,
I had imprinted on mind this clarity.
Losing myself in belonging to him,
Who hadn't promised belongingness.
Ascribing implications to silences,
Which very likely
Could adore meaninglessness.

Silences did actually speak much to me
Or was I over assuming?
True blows of honest time were soon to tell.
Everything else shouted loudly,
Yet he conceded through silence, ironically.
Only my dreams were heavenly,
Reality was as brutal as hell.

THE DARK

For me Dark has been
Peculiarly intriguing.
Why? Here are some reasons.
It's calm, yet chaotic.
It's lazy, yet hyper active.
It's colourless, yet colourful.
It's mysterious, yet beautiful.

It's the place where I met
Little Night Phlox gang.
Pinkish white smiles
At mid night hours of Dark,
Are bound to attract
Any tender heart.

Are you fearful of Light?
I naively asked.
Nah, it's that only

Dark gave us embrace.
We were too inferior
For Light's grace.

Ah! I too, fell for the Dark.
It's the place where I listened
Her outcast tales,
Her simple wishes,
Genuine thoughts,
Had on me some
Magical spell cast.

Don't you like Light?
I curiously asked.

Nah, I do but not more than Dark,
Light hadn't shown requisite courage
To accept my uniquely weird weirdness.
Ah! I too, dived in acceptance of dark.

It’s the place where I witnessed
His otherwise masked identity,
His open soul,
False promises,
His plain truths usually
Hindered behind guises.

Why can’t you be true in Light?
I, while shattering, asked.
Nah, I prefer to conceal in Dark.
Lights should see only what I permit,
Fabricated aura of goodness I like to build.
Ah! I too, was so thankful to Dark.

DEPRESSION

One of my hands is caught by it,
Being pushed away from light.
In my mind only
Thoughts of death, zero interest in life.
Flowers look at me,
Dwindle and die.
Moon has stopped visiting house of night.
I am consistently being pulled
Into an infinite void.
I want to strangle my own weak voice.

To me musical rhythms
Sound as shrill screams.
Down my cheeks tears roll
Like an infinite stream.
I don't wish to open my eyes.
Windows of my room,
I have closed too tight.

I begin to hate my own essence.
I pray for annihilation
Of this doomed existence.
I know no smiles.
Even birds generate only cries.
I am no longer called by mornings.
I no longer feel fascinated
By orange sight of evenings.

What is this all happening to me?
O Life! What are you exactly doing to me?
I find my soul living in a hell, caged.
I am neither alive
Nor embraced by death.
My mind can't recognize
My face in mirror.
I appear to my heart
As if some stranger.
This isn't me.
To this kind of fate's play,

I can't agree.

I can't accept such end of story.

Listen O Life! I do deny.

I still own wings, to attempt to fly.

I will effort hard until last breath,

To reach out at opening of this dark tunnel.

I need to convince my soul,

It is not an inescapable loop.

It is not indeed.

There is a wide way out

From this deep frenzy.

Depression is powerful,

But I do have a spirit.

I have bits of courage left in my baggage.

I have pieces of faith lying here and there.

Depression is sucking my blood,

Drop by drop.

But it has to surrender.

Because, of this battle, I am the winner.

FREEDOM

A veil drops from face of your love,
Emotions of my heart wide open their eyes,
See complete absence of love and cry,
Few more veils drop, reality is now free.

A rope breaks from across my fingers,
They move gently to wipe bundles of tears.
Dams of gloom taste freedom
And release all pain.
Joy has before it total space.

A piece of earth casts off steel shackles,
Softly travels its way to my burdened skin.
New cells, new tissues
Sprout from hidden seeds.
Life breathes freedom from slumbering.

Sails are free in ocean of existence,
To explore ports of happiness and glee.

DUST STORMS

I stand at centre of
A virulent storm.
Violent, making deadly sounds.
Big chunks of air
Rotate wildly around me.

This wild fellow inclined towards
Devastation, has no company of clouds;
Dark, grey or black,
No lightning, no downpour of arrows ,
Born of water.

It carries billions of dust bullets
In its baggage;
Blinding my eyes,
Blurring my path,
Burdening my little blooms to fall,
Destroying my garden

From lavish green to dead brown.

Yet, equally stubborn is my heart.
It waters grass' roots
Through its blood,
Lowers their heads,
Hardens their stems,
Soft leaves it sharpens into thorns.
There is never total destruction.

I keep standing head high
At centre of virulent storm.
I keep possessing a garden, garden of life.
Where thorns sustain life on their
Pointed edges and let resilient songs dance.

DARKNESS

Darkness that lingers before your eyes,
Engulfs you from all possible sides,
Pushes you towards death,
Obliterates life,
It's not really an obstacle as it seems.

Deadlocks it creates aren't ends,
Rather signals ,
Outward lights have dwindled down,
Rendered Inefficient.
Turn to your inner self, perennial source.
Find yourself there.
Find your light unaltered.

It will take time to reach at core.
Hold on to patience,
You won't get astray.
Universe conspires to clear your way.

Directs yours steps towards your soul.
There, whole life stays.

You may be overpowered
By dark for time being.
To conquer it is your ultimate destiny.
You have been blessed
With a promise unbroken.
Chains of agony, can't bound you.
You are meant for bliss's terrain.

Cast away spell of darkness.
Run, walk, crawl,
Move towards your inner heart.
That's the place
Where light of zillions of galaxies reside.
Undying presence, you were,
You are always in company with.
Undying light you are born with.

INCOMPLETE POEM

In the bottom most drawer of her table
Rests a half piece of paper;
Aged, bleak, yellowed yet loud,
It has scribbled on it an incomplete poem.

Poem about her clipped wings,
About her fanciful dreams,
About her life vision,
About her age long confinement.

A wonderful hard hitting paragraph
in it, radiates her grit, her determination.
How she is growing bit by bit,
Block by block, her torn wings.

To them who tried to kill her
Who wished to control her,
Make her a puppet,

She is sending befitting answers.

Each day she is adding
A powerful line to her incomplete poem.
And I with my breaths held
With excitement,
I'm eagerly waiting for its evolution.

VOID

Love, someday, I had in my heart.
I was covered head to toe in its embrace.
Life had seeped into my skin
And was living me, kissing each pore.
Love, once had
Complete ownership of my heart .
One day then, suddenly left,
Didn’t tell why?
Neither did allow me to seek answer.
It just left so quickly, at light's pace.
Emptiness ruled my heart for a time.
Laughing loudly there,
Rejoicing its monopoly.
New visitors came slowly, claimed authority.
Doubts, fears, lack of trust,
Vulnerabilities, many more,
Filling my heart's void as chain unbroken.
My cup is too full now upto the mouth.
I don’t love anymore.
I can’t love anymore.

SEEKING REALITY IN HIS WORDS.

I tended to seek reality,
In words he used to use.
Carefully articulated,
Preceded and followed by deliberate pauses
That were his bridles ,
If words happen to wander random ways.
Reality may be there, little not more.
More his words did hide,
Frank were only few.

I tended to seek reality,
In sparkle his eyes glitter.
Minute gestures,
Friendly eye-contacts,
Awkward take aways,
Eye-lids were his loyal slaves.
Quickly they maneuvered
Closing to conceal things

From coming into my notice.
Reality may be there, little not more.
His eyes didn't tell lies.
Truths they uttered few.

I tended to seek reality,
In silence he eventually left.
Completely sound-less it was.
No faintest echoes to listen.
Chaos runs in my brain.
To have a look at
His cautiously guarded deep,
Deep heart invariably has resulted
In nothing, but vain.

Love, I do hold for him
But I don't know
If he truly entertained feelings for me,
Any feelings.
If not more, may be few.

THE SUN AND THE MOON

Often on my way back home,
I notice tired Sun and energetic Moon
Sharing same stretch of blue.
Moments when buds are closing eyes
And leaves patting them to sleep,
Strings of air are embedded
With poesies serene.

But pale Sun and white Moon are silent.
I deeply believe they aren't,
They do talk.
Life of Moon is coming into being.
Life of Sun rolling into rest.
Sun must be telling his beautiful vision of
lovely Earth to the new guest, Moon;
Tales of beauty.

Moon seems amazed at descriptions of
What he is going to relish whole night.
He plays with vapours hung in space

And carefully places them
In the palms of sleepy leaves as cool dew;
His message for upcoming Sun.

Sun picks up dew drops one by one,
As a reader turns pages
Of an enchanting novel.
He smiles.
His rays touching wings
Of the butterflies softly.
He feels so content
As he looks at pastures
Through Moon's eyes.

STRENGTH

I fell in love,
Filled my whole heart,
Employed my full soul,
I got lost in love.

But love didn't stay,
Converted my heart
into powdered pieces,
Left scars on my soul.

I had no home,
I had no rest.
I was fighting with myself
In land of pain.

But I hold no regrets.
I am proud of my heart,
I am content with my soul

For, they have capacity to love.

I am not going to build any walls,
I am not going to hide in corners.
I still carry faith in my palms,
I still believe in love.

For it's only love
Of which we are made,
Through which we do breathe
And in the lap of which
We do live.

SILENCE

I fell in love with silence
Or silence fell in love with me,
I can't decisively conclude.
It is entirely true.
Most of times we can be found together.

Do I seek anything from silence?
Or is silence seeking something in me?
I doubt if it is anyway as such,
I remain blank in its company.
Nor it is interested
In strangest sort of words.
Both of us still do talk nuances.

World apprehends our association
In divergent manners, in different contexts.
When that disgusting allegation
Was unscrupulously thrown at me

And Silence engulfed me,
They thought I pleaded guilty.
Me too didn't try to bring them home.
What I was attempting was nothing more
Than safety of vulnerable dignities.

I don't mostly meet people alone.
I woo silence to come along with me.
What's the point of framing answers?
If questions are actually kind of convictions.
Courts of biased and prejudiced judges
Can't do justice to anyone, to me.

Sounds have long left my abode,
For reasons they didn't tell, I fear I know.
My love has worn silence.
My hatred has worn silence.
My insecurities, my anxieties
Have turned silent too.

When did I claim I am a perfect creature?

When did I expect

Pure perfection from You?

There was a moment

When you killed conversations.

There is a moment

When I choose silence though.

SEEKING ANSWERS

Answers dwell not in far-off land,
I know the address and directions.
Questions too are a bitter pain to handle.
Still I don't want to go there and seek,
I have no idea why.

Sometimes I feel I am fairly different
From that girl made her way in this city.
Changes have been registered
In appreciable quantity,
For good or bad I am in process to decide.
Is it growth or deterioration
I too want to find.

Memories haunt me,
The very ones bring a smile.
Desires and wishes hit back and forth,
Nights desire to sleep a lot

To get lost in imagination.
Then try to avoid sleep
Not to have dreams of infatuation.
Puppet have I become
Amidst this slurry of humiliation.

No charm do I entertain
Anymore for people,
Engrossed in petty calculations all the time.
My emotions are
Poorly weak in mathematics,
And I don't believe it isn't fine.
Gates are open for non diplomatic minds.

Biggest happiness turned out
To be the biggest lesson.
Spell got over,
Its effects managed sustained mention.
More than melancholy,
Twisted realities were unveiled.

As always prowess of articulation prevailed,
Will take a long time for me
To mend self-esteem.

A part of me has been
Somewhere relinquished,
For never to be found, ever to be seen.
Complete trust forwent
Its place in dictionary.
Tinges of doubts persist, remain stubbornly.
Love I may be able to fall in, perhaps.
But adulterated,
Shaped by practical testimonies.

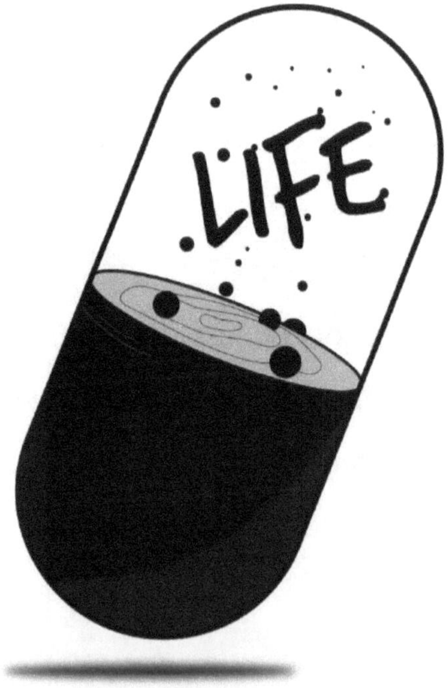
LIFE

WHOLE

Pure happiness or pure sadness,
Don't bestow me.
I like to relish mixed feelings.
Rainy eyes and blooming lips,
Simultaneously, at the same time.

Don't you agree.
It's neither day nor night.
Rather evening, mixed being,
That's more serene.
Light scatters down one shoulder of mine.
Dark begins to build its home on other.
I hold them both.
Made of both,
Not exclusively of one.

Isn't it more whole?
More multidimensional?

More conducive to growth?
A dried river bed or a flooded river,
Extremes aren't likeable.
Regulated flow lends helping hand
to vital crops to grow.

Don't throw me on edges, too extreme.
Overdose of agony might kill me.
Overdose of joy too.
Let my soul walk barefooted on all
Kinds of roads, rugged or smooth.
It might lose itself otherwise.

BLIND EYE

I can find no words,
I have no idea how to tell
How I got connected with her,
When I felt like being pulled towards her.

She, always struggling with
Her messed up hair,
Ultra loose jacket and dust particles,
Stubbornly sticking to her big glasses.

I used to watch her standing by the tea stall,
As she traversed the busy road.
Her time of arrival was fixed,
So was fixed her time of departure.

Besides was fixed
Her unusual bewilderment,
While she needed to cross noisy crossroad.

Her book swirling in her hands,
Her feet pressing hard against surface.

My eyes without a failure stuck at her.
Everyday it took almost thirty minutes
To her to cross that point,
Which I thought was
Not so difficult to cross over.
Why was her puzzlement?

She never looked scared,
There were no signs of fearfulness.
Otherwise she walked light on road
With earphones pouring music in her ears.

One day I somehow managed courage
To ask her if I could help her
To get through that devil like crossroad.
Her pretty innocent smile said a yes.

'I just get a bit of confusion,'
Reaching at the other end she said.
'You know this naughty blind eye of mine
Behaves a little difficult.'
Uttering thanks she left.

My mind was still visualizing her eyes.
Round black deep, holding beauty.
One of them though was blind,
Her words were echoing in airs.

And now I wait at appointed times
To catch her hands,
Amidst jumbled noise
Hovering at crossroad.
She doesn't talk about it but
I am sure she knows
I love her.

CHOICE: LIFE OR DEATH?

Years I have lived and cherished,
Company of Life.
I haven't chosen it,
Albeit I tried to handle it tenderly,
When it was put into my palms.

Colours, songs, melodies, forms,
How much it has shown to my intellect.
Black, white and grey , objectively
It has forced me to go through.
It said its desire is to see me grow.

Branches expand,
Flowers blown,
Seeds spread,
But I miss the roots;
Core of my being.
Life blows winds that carry me away.

I want to turn back, I say.

Death smiles at me
From other edge of horizon.
Promises me a return.
I employ my brains on work.
Life counter attacks.
Beware! It's death's illusion.

It won't take you to place serene.
It might desert you midway.
Where you would lose
Your deserved pathway.
I have to make a choice.
Death's embrace or
Some more time with life.

Life could bring me only this far.
Neither it knows how to hold me,
How to calm me, how to quench my thirst,

Nor how to answer my quest.

For years I have been a being.
What I am seeking now is non-being.
Death insists it can fulfil my longing.
What should be my choice,
I think it's too obvious,
Decisively tilting.

COLOUR OF SILENCE

I think colour of Silence is Orange.
Not pure, mixed with pieces of yellow,
Blue holds and resonate sounds,
And dark isn't silence.
It's annulment of voices.

Silence isn't destruction of Sound.
Rather a carrier of much deeper sound
That is beyond ears,
But intelligible to a Soul deeply in Love.

As Day recedes,
It paints Blue with Orange
For few moments.
Shallow sounds submerged
Under deeper depths.
Feel the calmness transcending
Down through your Soul.

Words attain real meanings at these times.
Meanings that reach Soul
But can't be expressed.
Heart doesn't pump blood albeit a rhythm,
That is closer to substance of Life.

A DIFFERENT KIND OF SKY

I wish for a sky that is different from
This blue umbrella smiling over my head.
I don't say I don't like it,
It's amazing.
It embraces everything.
It doesn't know discrimination.

Snowy white clouds play in its lap.
Thunder impregnated black storms too
Get a huge space to scroll over.
Blue humbly recedes to allow setting sun to
Paint yellow orange abstract things.
It doesn't leave hands of Sun,
Even when it's disappearing
Helplessly under west burden.

It gives rainbows.
It rains when I cry.

It is home of Moon.

It gives equal importance to faintest stars.

It opens arms for those nights too ,

That are just dark

Not embellished with glittery glows.

It's so likeable.

Still I wish for a different sky.

I have only one reason.

It knows how to carry sounds.

Voices hit my head like rudest of hammers-

A chaos, a noise.

A chunk taking me away from substance

Of silence that forms core of my soul.

I want a sky that is simply Silent.

TIME

You say nothing is in
Life to make it worthy to live.
Your eyes speak language of deep ache,
Your heart is constantly pumping despair.

You are broken.
You seem like an epitome of disbelief.
It is understandable.
It is evident;
Your fears, your vulnerabilities,
Your insecurities.

But you aren't destined
To be forever like this.
You have turned yourself
Slave of yesterdays.
You have allowed callous time to bind,
You have made time your master.

It isn't real truth.

You are the Lord of your moments.

Identify yourself.

Assume reigns in your own hands.

Ride over time's tides.

Write your tomorrows

With complete authority.

Life is worthy to live.

In thick jungles of despair,

Hope does dwell.

Free yourself.

Defeat time's deadly soldiers.

You are here to win.

You will win.

I AM A STREET CHILD

My definition of home I say so proudly,
Is very broad indeed.
It's not a four-walled structure
Demarcated by a secure iron boundary.
It's not a locked accumulation of stones
Where breezes of any kind,
Need permissions of doors
Or windows for entry.

I am a street child as they call me.
In my autobiography
I can't mention very basic facts about me.
I didn't go to school
To learn about diverse seasons.
I have felt them very closely.

They term me deprived.
I disagree.

I own so much.
I have stocks of breaths in my chest.
I have streams of courage,
Flowing in my blood.
My dawns begin with struggles,
My dusks end up thirsty.
Yet, I own a night
Decorated by lamps quite starry.

I welcome life as it comes to me.
Cruel, I don't call it.
To be kinder, I don't plead it.
In my childhood,
I am living as an adult.
Scars on my palms and wounds on my feet,
Don't incline to curse life as hell.

Naked realties I have seen.
I myself became vendor
Of masks needed so badly.

What is this innocence,
I am oblivious of its meaning.
Here I am deprived,
But I am sailing through Life.

They try to push me towards death.
They want me to sell death.
From where I have no idea,
But I know life's value.
I deny to be servile.
I may not be a carefully reared rose.
I will bloom as a wildflower
Under sky's canopy.

RAPE

Horrors of that day are vitally alive
Six years old, I was an innocent child.
Living in my own beautiful world
Unaware of how brutalities roam here.
My soft gentle limbs were violated,
I had no idea with me what had happened.
My body was in immense pain.
I had never felt such strain
Uncle pressed fingers against my lips,
Don't sob, don't scream,
Don't tell to anyone.
He took me back my home
Without a bit of guilt.
I scrolled in my bed whole night, aching.
Breathless, even today
They keep me waking.
Numb, as I rush to wash my face
I see in mirror

That six years old boy engulfed by fear.

WORLD OF LOVE

I dream of a world
Created of elements of love,
Where joys and pains
Will be nothing but products of love,
To be relished under auspices of,
To be cured through dosages of,
Love.

I don't wish for complete calm,
Chaos is important for
Relative importance of calmness though.
In clamours of heart piercing negativities,
Love will not take back its positive hold.
I simply harbour such hopes.

I dream of pretty exquisite flowers
Making my place their fragrant home.
Of course they will have to undergo

Harsh forces of autumns
To make waits of springs worth.
Blooms and decay will come naturally.
Messengers of love won't be ever crushed.

Acceptances will reign
Over judgements there.
Cages will not be able
To cage freedom of love.
I dream of a world
Where I won't be compelled
To live only my half-soul.
Darkness will also exist there.
But my other half of soul
Will enjoy its light, its due share.

LOVE AND NAMELESSNESS

When they asked for a name
To name this love that has
Penetrated my heart's each cell,
I couldn't tell either.
Then, they named me a sinner.

Namelessness is heretical.
It smells of unscrupulousness.
Unregulated, without laws,
It's a blot on moral order.
Negative, it defies boundaries.
It is evil.

My head nods.
Uninterested in arguments,
It reverts back to itself.
Namelessness isn't impure.
It worships Love in its purity.

It looks beyond boundaries towards
Land of lights shining eternally.

It has no rigid standards.
It has no fatal formulations.
It isn't true.
Righteousness it respects.
It hails acceptance,
Only judgements it does move away from.

It isn't a denial.
It's where my love blooms
And evolves continuously.
No promises, no expectations
Here I have to offer.
But a wider embrace
That's trying to be wider.

Your vulnerabilities
Won't be exploited here.

Your scars won't be disallowed to heal.

Neither you need to conceal,

Your fears, your insecurities.

Nameless is my love,

Where singularly Love owns hegemony.

TO MY DADA (ELDER BROTHER)

Life of mine is imbalanced
On practical side.
Will remain so I believe.
Weirdness is my real name.
All I have is just ill fame.

I wasn't surprised,
That's why when during our first meeting
I had nothing,
But a bad impression
On your mind about me.
Things were different though on my side.

I saw a light,
A light wrapped in peace.
I saw a solace,
That was being radiated towards me.
I heard a voice that had utter familiarity.

I didn't know you.

You weren't stranger yet, for me.

Little things grew in empty space.

I was welcomed where I had such a place.

Breaking barrier of times,

Busiest hours took halt to listen to my grief.

I got an address where I could run to weep.

I wasn't offered an easy hand

To cross my crossroads.

I was furnished with maps and tools

To find my own safe course.

And I can share what haunts me,

When I collapse and do wish to die.

Because I know,

You on the other side are listening.

I don't agree easily.

I am doubt solely.

Meagre belief.
You on the other side continue listening.
Value my petty stupid talking.

From deep darkness here I effort to rise.
Since you exhort me to fight,
My chaotic storms find
Calming note in your face.
I know I would live.
I know I won't die.

And I would like to believe,
One day I be doing stuff
I have been sent into this world for.
And then I would be recalling
My lost self, its bewilderment.
And write few words to you -
Dear Dada, Thank You.

DO I CRY FOR YOU?

Do I cry for you until now?
If so for what reasons?
Destiny has etched conviction,
You don't belong to me.

In fact you never did.
I was not in ignorance.
Knew it well,
You were of someone else.

I believe that wasn't love.
I didn't love you, I don't.
From where do tears
Derive their source? I wonder.

No rights on you I have.
Isn't missing you invalid then?
Don't I keep your memories

Like some illegal treasure?

At times I think I continuously lie
To my soul, push my heart to hide,
Feelings it lived in their deepest essence.
It murmurs it's love indeed.

How could I love you?
Throwing myself in oceans
Of pains and pains deliberately.
How could I choose such insanity?

But, I can't alter reality though.
Doesn't matter what it really was.
Agony in my heart beats the only truth:
Dreams are always in hurry to pass.

JUDGEMENTS

When I express my intent
To disagree from their argument,
Concerns give way to judgment.
Analysis lead contrary to acceptance.

Hedge their hopes,
Still they effort to cut unwanted parts away.
Loose soil I am? To lend any shape.
Tightly they grip not to let escape.

To begin with, I quietly watch this exercise.
Amused at their ardent wish
To make me deprived,
Of opinions I hold in contrast
To their suiting.
Troublesome it is, don't they find it tiring?

Slowly I retire from such place
In quest for some healthy solace.
Not that I am dogmatic kind of being.
I do like to mend my illogical thinking.

Cannot allow though sheer imposition,
I would like to go as per my disposition.
These frequent events remind me of thee.
How you allowed space for individual me.

Much of my stuff was
Sheer opposite to your liking.
Yet, you freed me to learn
By trails and erring.
Those manners of interaction
Couldn't go for long
Alas! To my bad luck
You didn't have that patience strong.

Your leaving the scene was a hard setback,

I embarked on reviewing entire life track.
Wrong may be I;
Without truth having been found.
Still coercion can't be legitimized;
How this principle isn't sound?

Lone I am; having no one to support.
But can't say flattering YES
Just to manage rapport.
Can't learn skills to succumb to hegemony.
Messy may be, I would love
To discover my own harmony.

MEMORIES

A bizarre song occupies
Its somewhat forced place in my mind,
This very silent night.
That is broken by occasional rustling
Of green and dry leaves,
Helpless under powerful
Sway of moody winds.
My memory channels could recollect
Only half of the lyrics,
Remaining half lost under
Reckless dust storm of mighty time.
And I feel my soul fully filled up to the brim
Of restlessness and anxiousness
Of missing a bond,
That I wished to
But never could actually be formed.
Silent night sings highly strange melody
To sway me to the lands where he lives,

Having whom was the thing I wished.
My eyes lose all the control
And tears gush out
On silent rhythmic notes to dance.

WORDS

My words and I do share
An uncanny relation.
I, overfilled with emotions,
They, loving emotionless notions.

It's not any sort of surprise
That for large measures of time we fight.
Pen moving right and left in my fingers,
Words refusing to appear on paper.

I want to write about love:
Its charm, its warmth,
Joyous days, happy nights,
Words give me a weird look and
Pile themselves up in form of a book.

Then they slowly dance on cover page
And scrawl their favourite title

On empty space.
"Detachment," is what
They are obsessed about.
"Emotions," I cry aloud.

They keep dancing as if
They don't listen.
My words and I do share
Highly uncanny relation.

RIPPLES

Ripples adorn hidden secrets of seas
Way too beautifully.
Zig-zag motion, melodious frequencies,
Cover tactically, what's lying underneath.

A fierce fire, that's burning its own chest.
Fumes of agony it emits.
There is a turbulence
Dissolved in deep silence.
Restlessness prevails here in voicelessness.

Her face aptly assumes this simile.
Ripples of charming smiles
Veil sensations of melancholy
That run through her heart.
Pauses between her breaths
Are replete with stories.

Dark tales of treatment inhumane
Are hidden in unreachable corners
Of her soul,
Guarded well by her infectious smiles.
How much she holds untold,
To fathom I often try.

No one could, but know.
She has made herself inaccessible.
She is too skilled: adept highly.
Misunderstood, misjudged,
Never tasted acceptance.
She is unknown even to mirror of her own.

BOUND TO BE PERFECT

You hide your heart, employ manoeuvres.
Use most indirect symbols possible
To negate imperfections
That are part of yours,
To create an image.

Your soul is crafted of most perfect
Material of the cosmos: it's so bright.
Dark patches you are too cautious of,
Are temporal stages of its growth
Towards meeting its own self.

Don't cover them up.
Don't be shy of your faults.
Don't be ashamed of your failures.
Work on them.
Use best of tools called wisdom.

Lay your heart bare open.
It need not be all white for Love
To knock at its left or right door.
Love loves the path through which
Soul evolves in
The direction of pure existence.

Shed off diplomatic tactics,
Shed off this infatuation
For an image good.
Let real love come
To real you and embrace you.
You are bound to be Perfect.

UNCERTAINTY

Life is sitting next to me
As I am staring at the sun,
Going to hide in the sky.
Morning gives space to evening,
Evening yields field to night
And after night hours,
Sun again.
I am thinking a fixed cycle.
Definite. Certain.

I turn my face towards life
And break the silence between us.
Why is my destiny so uncertain?
Why are my ways so hazy?
Why are my Moons
So unsure of next night?
Why do my Suns shiver in fright?
My past is bleak.

My present is tired.
My future lingering at edge of death.

Life takes a deep breath.
My poor Life, more tired than me,
Because of awful mistakes I have done.
Yet, It has no remorse.
It has committed breaths,
It steals everyday from clutches of death.
It knows not whether it would live.
It will, it just believes.
It slowly whispers in my ears.

Just wait, wait my dear.
Paint the moments you have.
Knowing much future won't either help.
This uncertainty has its own bliss
Where don't you see you are
Strengthening more and more
Your hard resilience.

Keep crafting your painting,
Why do you bother!
Let time and death
Fight over place of their meeting.

THEY DON'T KNOW US

They don't know about us,
We are continuous wanderers.
In our world, definitions are fluid,
With dogmas we don't live.

We enjoy things simple.
Simple joys of life,
Normally taken so usual.
No toxic flavours of money or power.

There aren't tricky jargons.
They can know about us.
If they wish to talk to their hearts
And have a look at their souls.

We don't talk about a world, alien.
We are trying to be more human.
We don't shut out dissenting voices.

We allow ideas to clash in search of Truth.

We are striving for rule of love.
We tend to replace
Judgements by empathy.
They term us heretic.
They say we want to disrupt order.

They refuse to acknowledge force of love.
They choose to be blinded
By glitters of gold unreal.
We only work to spread love on earth.

Souls are here to bloom.
To erupt scents.
To taste humming of laborious bees.
To evolve, to grow.

Which cuts roots from
Vital source of water is a sin.

We aren't seeking destructions.

We are wanting a world of lively, free souls.

LET ME

Why are you letting fear and despair
Knocking at your door to come in?
Turn a bit and have a look at your window
Where I am standing.
Don't you know you aren't alone?

Your shoulders are empty
But your heart is carrying a burden.
You hate light,
Dark has become unusually pleasant.
It's okay, but you can't shun radiance;
That resides in your soul.
Broken you are feeling,
You carry inside a brilliant world, whole.

Let me take your hands
And show you the mirror,
Reflections of life there glitter.

They aren't unreal.
You and I- we aren't homeless,
We are on a journey back to our homes.
Rugged rocks, piercing stones,
Still lot of stories are left untold.

If you will to choose silence,
Don't choose usual wordless one,
But that which leads to music.
A few songs do I know,
I know you would join me, to sing.
Rhythms of cheers
At the centre of realms of gloom,
I am sure we can fake out curse
As some boon.

Don't say NO to life's tricks,
Surrender is heavy, much more than
Breaths that burn the very chest.
If you can't be strong in conventional sense,

Don't worry, be you.
You are walking and you have a path.
Definitely you are going to reach the end.

End that isn't east or west
But where dwell purple sunsets.
Serene breezes pass through you
Touching your essence.
And where you can close your eyes
And forget your mind,
After life's harsh battle
You are thus entitled to rest,
In arms of green yellow seas
Where bliss gets slowly unleashed.

YOU ARE NOT ALONE

Ripples of melancholy and anxiety
Persistently wash off your heart's peace.
Your fragile worn out boat
Push hard to sail through,
As they hurl their narrow,
Biased judgements at you.

It sometimes seems adversities will succeed,
And quash staggering life,
Arduously attempting to breathe.
It's sometimes feared gushes of
Errant waves may get you broken
And you choose to sink deep
Without breath, in realm of death.

But I know you my dear Friend,
I know your everlasting wounds
Can never succeed.

And you won't succumb to their trap.
I know cracks on your soul
May ache to worst extent possible,
But you will never pray
For redeeming easy death.

Don't feel yourself alone my rfiend,
On this huge spread of blue.
It's so uncertain here, its calmness a myth,
Glued into violent blows.
But I want to say to you, I want to tell you,
My love for you will stay forever.
It will ride over all temporariness,
To dwell in islets of resilient association.

Don't feel so chaotic at heart,
Come lay your head over my chest,
And let me ask your silence about
Hard times when they tried to demean you,
Or about deliberate acts

They did to cancel you out.
Let me take you to place
Of simple acceptance,
My soul is rooted into.

I understand it's difficult, way too difficult,
But trust me as I trust you.
Life has been harsh,
It may continue to be harsh too.
Allow me to share drops of pain
From your cup.
And pour juice of joy from mine into yours,
Not for any lofty complex reason.
Just because I love you.

IT'S YOUR CORE TOO

Misty drops endeavour to keep
Beloved leaves for long in their embrace.
They wish to pour out their essence
Gradually over glossy skins,
To have green veins imbibe
Love and care sourced from floating hearts.

Love exhibiting itself
In any form pure is serene.
It heals eyes.
It heals chaotic senses.
It heals doomed parts of nomadic souls.
It pushes me more towards my own self.

Waters move up from beneath
Several miles of earth to run into rooms.
Waters effort to reach zenith of skies
To fall and to hug blooms.
Waters remain awake as steady dew

In laps of restless sleepless leaves.

Why so?
Why this hard work?
Why to stretch beyond own textures
Undertaking attempts so arduous.
It's the atom of love and affection
Out of which entire cosmos is created.

Don't be surprised.
It's your core too.

CHRONIC PAIN

Sleepless nights visit you daily,
Stars and moon have faded in your sky,
Tears roam around your eyelids,
Silently you cry.
Your summers have turned cold.
Springs have damaged your garden.
Memories flood your heart with pain,
You try your best
But they simply don't listen.
You feel you are weak,
You think you are not worthy to live.
Don't be harsh on yourself dear.
Don't blame yourself badly
For this chronic pain.
You haven't done anything wrong,
You just loved.
What if none know
How you are going through,

I assure you, you will survive my friend.

Aches and cuts of broken Love,

My friend, I do understand.

WORDS YOU WRITE

Words you write accuse me
For crushing your heart.
As a sinner you portray me.
I read them in my lone corner
At dark nights and try to force
Tears not to come out of my eyes.

Complaints your words hold
Invariably in every stroke.
Ah, but the pauses in between
From everyone else t
They may remain concealed.
They pierce my soul, sharpest of knives.
I do feel.

I can't say it's unjust to me, no.
Anger rushed at me, well deserved indeed.
I realise what you had to go through,

What I did.

While protecting my own nest I failed to see

How many times you would get killed

At hands of torture-some queries.

To face you on some unplanned occasions,

Fills me with weird anxieties.

I remember how you compelled

That shaking smile

To stick amid melancholies,

Your soul is actually burdened under.

Made me sink

More and more in repentance.

I don't plead for clemency, not worth it.

Each night I punish myself

Reading your poetry.

Resentment, sobbings,

Your tender untainted emotions

That I recklessly crushed,
Couldn't show bravery.
Even today I can't acknowledge
Your presence without hesitation.

Sorry I am, for becoming the cause
That taught you what means destruction.
Never wished so,
Couldn't anticipate small things
Can acquire huge harm,
If not taken into concern
Due to mind's fluctuation.
Guilty I am of spoiling your innocence.
Remedies I don't have,
Can only push myself
To imbibe your torments.

RESTLESS MOMENTS

Moments that are most restless for me
Are specifically those
When thoughts cloud my mind,
But words leave abode of my soul
To wander in dark thickets
Of barren forests.

In these moments I feel more than normal,
Emotions of all sorts
Occupy my lonesome heart,
Exhibit to the fullest extent virulent force,
Fully aware of happenings, I find myself
Attacked,
Still can't spill out pain in form of words.

Helplessness grows upon me hurriedly,
Speedily I entice and exhort words
To please come back

To render me respite of a moment or two.
Bless me with fragments of peace,
May be very few.

They refuse to return,
What harm have I done?
Through time I have been a devout lover,
Offered stipulated sacrifices,
Practised prescribed rituals,
Never missed necessary customs.

I plead, plead and plead a return
Vanished among fuming storms,
I wait for a boat of rescue,
Making myself competent for words,
Again.

NAMELESS STORMS

Questions walk in my head,
Steady, rigorous steps.
I haven't placed them in any category.
You say they blatantly touch edges of heresy.

I am neither shocked nor surprised.
I am fairly used to.
For every categorization pulls me
Towards negative territory of boundary.

I am still nameless.
I don't see reality.
I don't see illusions.
I am stuck in between.
From where I tend
To tread beyond everything.

But they can't satisfy my thirst.
Storms rattling in my mind
Don't contain water droplets.
They only thunder and pour
Lightening to pierce me.

I don't look for a shore
To convince things to rest.
I look for centre of ocean,
To collect water
And impregnate their dry wombs.

Divine rains in closets of my brains
Will light a tranquility:
Formless, shapeless, flexible,
Devoid of rigidity.
I can proclaim,
Peace holds namelessness
In its closest vicinity.

IDENTITY

They look at us
In unusual manners.
They outrightly term us
As abnormals.

We don't fit in
Their rigid patterns.
Our existence defies
Their ideas of gender.

Stigma, exclusion,
Abuse, trauma,
Physical and mental harassment,
Multiple things we are forced to face.

But we aren't ashamed of us,
Our identity we proudly embrace.
We have hearts, souls and brains.

We too can walk on life's normal ways.

We are here to live, to love, to dance,
To sing, to write, to read.
We are as human as you are.
We are as mortal as you are.

We respect your sense of gender,
We ask you to respect our sense too.
We too dream to taste life,
We too dream to fly high,
Just like you.

MIRROR

Your words vividly echo,
"You won't be able to see
Yourself in mirror, let aside people."
That you did, emptied on my face
Whole bottle of acid.

My screams occupied my ears.
Burns, cuts, innumerable stitches,
My reflection in the mirror
Had turned into deadly horror.

I had done nothing wrong to you.
I had only chosen my right to say No.
You forcefully tended
To assert your fake ego.
You desired revenge.

You thought my beauty,
My strength dwelled in my face.
You thought you could
End my life this way.
You thought you could put me down.
Torn me away.

My soul isn't tainted.
My soul is brave.
Instead of lying down,
It has risen up again.
My soul knows well how
To not fall, how to sustain.

Yes, I cried for days.
Yes, my heart ached for days.
Yes, I was immersed in immense pain.
Yes, I was hit physically and mentally.
Yes, in moments I felt like dead.

Yet, my soul generated spirit to win.
I am not only living, I am happily living.
Mirror isn't anymore my enemy,
I cherish my face and its beauty.

MY EMPTY SOUL

My heart is filled with heavy beats.
My chest with breaths that so laboriously
Drag themselves over footpath of life.
My mind is brimming with thoughts,
Some too uncanny, some too absurd.
That's why I have long believed-
My soul must have been
A home of permanent chaos.
But I find it empty.
Blood has leaked via
Crevices dug by wounds, gifted by love.
Deprived of life it is ,
Unwanted also to death.
It neither lives nor is dead.
It neither is caged nor freed.
It is hugged ,
Warmly and tightly by emptiness.
No music. No words.

No sobbing. No cry.

Albeit a yearning for its source.

A desire that keeps pushing it backwards.

PROMISE

Amusing it is how we both know
Promises you subscribe to
Are like winter snow,
Destined to disappear in concrete form
As summer comes with its weapons warm.

You blink your eyes and say I will,
My mind smiles and you well sense it,
Still you keep avowing,
I keep believing, you or me,
Whom who is deceiving.

Autumn in our world knocks frequently.
For it we have developed a habit uncanny.
I blame skies, you point to whims of destiny
Why do we conceal lack of your own will?

Flowers wither with time inevitably,
Don't try to make me trust contrarily.
Tell the truth you want to leave, don't lie.
Thing that isn't in existence can't die.

You don't love me, I am aware wholly.
Don't compel yourself to show reciprocity.
Your denials won't shatter my heart,
More than your forged promises do.
Don't choose silence.
Say the truth.

HER

I might have been a deadly warrior,
Winning battles and acclaims.
Tears well up in her eyes
And sword in my hand shakes.
Her muscles shiver.
Body bit by bit decimates.
More and more helpless,
It renders me perplexed.

What's the use of long shiny sword
Swirling in my hands?
What's the value of victory medals
Crowding my chest?
She plainly crosses flames of pain.
I arduously try to avert but in vain.

My beats are fraction of hers,
My breaths too.

She is my substance,
My very life force.
I sit in a corner and see her struggling.
How badly I feel to alter everything, totally.

My mind is bewildered.
I wander for solutions.
They evade brazenly.
I come at the verge of getting shattered.
Her eyes carry a glimmer.
She whispers, "You are a warrior.

"GRANDFATHER

In my moments of utter despair in life,
My feet involuntarily take me to the room
Located in the last corner of my house.

Solitude lives here joyfully.
Sun brilliantly sets at its large window.
Parting yellow rays hug each other tightly.

Little sparrows have their small nest
In upper edge of wooden door.
A happy family toils and chirps happily.

This room has something
More special for me.
A rack of five shelves.
A few figurines have occupied
The top most floor authoritatively.

Bottom four shelves
Contain hardcover diaries
Written by my late grandfather.
In his lap I have played as an infant
But have no live memories.

He caresses me yet.
Pages of my birthday
Spill his pure happiness.
But large number of them
Portray stories of his struggles.

Stories of wide disappointments,
Betrayals, losses.
Even there were points where he had
Nothing to hold on and survive.

But he did.
He did go through.
He won.

He lost.
He won again.
Never gave up.
His life, a plethora of tests.

He faced everything.
His head proudly up.
No tone of complaining gestures
I find in his diaries.

He isn't with me physically in this world.
Yet, he is the one with whom I talk when
I feel I am getting out of life stuff.

He used to cuddle three years old me.
His affectionate presence sustains me
When life pushes me off the cliff
And I feel falling.

Baba why you had to suddenly leave
I don't know.
Baba you know your absence
Is a vacuum so painful.
Baba, I need you.

Baba, I need you gently
Putting your hands on my head
And whispering, “My child don't worry.
I am here.
I am beside you.
I am with you.”

Sun is ritually setting at large window.
Bundles of sounds are emerging
From home of sparrow.
Your 1998 diary is smiling.

Drops of tears
Are rolling down my cheeks.

But words of your pages are echoing,

I am not weak.

Baba, you provide me enormous strength.

Your granddaughter will surely make it.

LIVING WITHOUT A FAKE LOVE.

What if fate didn't will things
I feel now were in my favour.
What if you had stayed,
Fully maintaining magic of
Fake love you had created around me.
A world where spring was
Repeatedly promised and were
Promised cool rains of togetherness,
At times autumn
Began to come into existence.

Carrying a whole pond of love
Inside my heart,
I might be seeing life
With two blind eyes.
I might be seeking delight in a light
That was composed of darkness.
Songs of soulless lyrics might have

Continued to echo in my closed walls,
That were of the belief
Of having large windows,
Letting in fresh airs.
But that were actually rotten.

I have no idea how time worked,
Planning it with acumen
Or doing it at sudden jerk.
Yes, I was broken, dejected, and thought
I will never be freed of loneliness.
Because you were Love for me.
You were Life.
Distance from you meant just death.

But today when
I remove curtains to inhale sunlight,
I am enriched by a feeling.
Feeling of being saved at right turn from
Love that was its most distorted version.

I am coming to learn love lives
In close neighbourhood of truth.
It ushers us in a land
That isn't dreamy
But nurturing real roots of life.
To witness how
Most beautiful flowers bloom
While thorns keep besieging them.

HUMILITY

You have tiny power in your hands.
You think others are weak.
You know one extra word.
You say others are dumb.

A meagre tag of superiority,
And you don't allow anyone
To sit in front of you while you talk.
Others don't deserve.

I ask myself,
Do you believe yourself to be a human?
You are solely Ego:
Caged brain, idle heart, no love.

Power is like a flickering candle.
A strong blow of time,
It will be dead.
Power is like a roaming butterfly;
Will migrate from your garden,

If any other did a commendable
Job to allure it with better flowers.
Knowledge might rain over dumb
If he forces his blood to evaporate.

Your ego that is boosting you today,
Will embark upon killing you then.
You won't be able to resist.
You have made yourself a slave.

Don't listen to ego.
It's not worthy of being a guide.
It misleads away from life.
It brings destruction in guise of prosperity.

Learn to be humble.
Be grateful.
Dwell in your heart where love resides.
Be human, more human.
Be unaffected
By temporary whims of night.

DIGNITY

At one meeting
On a pre-decided day,
Held at southern most
Edge of the universe,
Were present
Stars, Moon and Sun.

As open discourses began and went on,
Taking an unwanted diversion,
Raged Sun mocked calm Moon.
Because Moon had raised a point,
Along with a few stars, disliked by Sun.
Sun thought it was
An attack on its domination.

So Sun ridiculed Moon,
Attacked at its dignity.
Shouting loudly Moon

Had nothing of its own.
Moon's beauty was owned to him
As by his light, Moon's dark home was lit.

Moon didn't lose his calm,
Neither his rational line of arguments.
He presented his convictions,
Though remained open for alterations.
He wasn't owner of his light he accepted,
But added he was in possession
Of equal dignity.

As a member of the vast universe
Each and everyone has his place,
His role to fulfill, his duties to do,
His natural spirit, his point of view.
And each and everyone is necessary,
Equally important, for things to grow.

JOURNEY

When God gifted me
Magical sparkles of life,
He said it's going to be
A journey so beautiful,
You will have darks
Interspersed between lights,
You will have internal strife,
Ups and downs,
But hope will keep dancing
In chirping of birds' songs.

Buds will transform themselves into flowers:
Red, blue and many other colours
To fill pores of your brown skin
With fragrances enchanting.
But after reaching a peak point,
They will wither too.
This is a rule no one can undo.

As also the other one,
New petals come alive
At place of vanishing buds.

Throughout my road
On life's hazy territory,
I attempted to keep myself focussed
At god's these sayings.
So inevitably there dawned nights
That were long unusually.
My soul hold me
On track of patience
Reminding for ultimate arrival
Of bright clear mornings,
Nights themselves provide
Solemn testimony.

And I walk adoring equally,
Tears in my eyes that symbolize phases low.
As I do like smiles playing

Merrily on my face,

Entreating me to join musical flow.

My heart reposits emotions tender,

It loves, gets hurt, suffers negative blows.

Yet, it does store a solid resilience

In its very core.

These breaths move

In a land of contradictions,

Where never promised were static skies,

Heavy angry clouds frequently

Hover in armies huge,

Pouring big drops of continuous hostilities.

But this is the required pre condition

For seven sisters of rainbows to approach,

And unravel serene beauty

Accompanying in background

Hummings of butterflies of all hues.

And so I walk cherishing
Permanent energy within;
Relishing transient character
Of outside world.
Death is inevitably waiting for me
At this or that turn,
Albeit diversity of trees decorating
And soothing the wayside,
Is made to bestow me
Black-white experience.

For full attainment of potential of soul,
Existence of evil is also necessary.
Stumbling over stones reveals
For opting a different trajectory,
Not always edgy stones are hurdles.
They become media
To forge rippling of waves,
That carry messages
From ocean's deep heart.

Silence and voices both create chaos,
Both generate a slew of queries.
Extreme restlessness inflicted upon mind
Leads it towards source of serenity.
Why to fear bad as it is
Just a precursor of good.
God never offered benign mountains
But put in skills of sculpting tools.

Nothing is here without beauty's trace.
Train your eyes well, don't let yourself fail.
Write a story however
bizarre it might seem.
Just inhale life's existence,
Have yourself enriched,
God is fascinated already
To hear your words,
After you enter his home successfully
Crossing rocky terrains.

WHO ARE YOU?

Who are you, standing at door
Willing to embrace me? I ask.
Don't you see my ugly scars?
You reply a yes and stick to your decision.
I wonder in a bewilderment.

Love, you can't be.
It had cut me deep into heart's centre,
I remember.
It wasn't blind,
Had eyes to cognize unworthy constituents
I am composed of.
It had left me with thick shades
Of scorn on its face.
You, ready to embrace.
Can't be Love, who are you?

Doors are tightly closed.
Had I done this?
I am insane deriving life from chains,
In between four huge walls.
Don't I desire to break free? I do.
I wish to cast a hefty smile
On persistent scars of past,
Unruly occupying a big place in present,
And tread along with soul
And my cracked heart.
I do.
How do you know?
Who are you?

Do you have knowledge of my name,
My home, my insecurities,
My broken music, my life and
Its grave I had built years ago?
You say you aren't oblivious and
Your eyes don't lose pieces of peace.

Are you really Love?

How can you be?

LOVE WITH YOU

I might not have fallen
In love with you.
But it's you who
Have poured shiny flow of
Love into my pen's nib.
My heart might not have
Yearned for you as
It thinks of Love.
But my poesies run
Towards you without a fail,
When they endeavour to touch Love.

I might not have seen
You as an essence ,
When I futilely attempt to define Love.
But my imagination sticks at you ,
Whenever I attempt to do so.
I might have never crafted

A home dreaming to live
In calm embraces of yours,
But my closed eyes don't
Visualize any seashore
That is savouring sun set without you.

What is this bond tying me to you?
Where I am attached with you,
Without being connected to you.
My heart doesn't beat
In tune with your heartbeats.
My voiceless eyes don't understand
wordless silence radiating from yours.
But when nights arrive
To capture sky's realms,
I don't see Moon but you.
But when birds sing
Exquisite songs at dawn
To welcome Ball of Fire,

I don’t feel warmth of Sun rather

I feel you.

WELCOME LOVE

Sorry, my room is a bit untidy
It's a bit dark, air is less here.
Oh! flowers have withered in vase blue,
Yellow papers are haphazardly scattered.

Please come dear Love, don't go.
I have waited for these seasons just for you.
Give me few seconds I will clean it up,
Drops of orange light will swarm in,
Let me open this rugged window.

Sit on the chair,
I will bring you a cup of coffee,
See what miracle you have brought
To rotten life tree.
Spring will eventually bloom with you,
I had belief.
Welcome Love, my stains have been

Badly for beautiful relief.

Only you can make me feel
I am a human being.
I have been crafted of you,
Only you have power
To render life fulfilling.
Take me with you where my real abode is,
My heart, my soul, my restless breaths
Have been awaiting for long,
For peace in your embrace that is.

CRUEL TOWARDS MYSELF

Voices of my pierced heart condemn me.
I run madly for safe refuge
Away from questions badly disturbing me.
Nights tell,
There is no refuge, no home, no peace.

Foolish I am, have committed blunders.
Have neglected wise things,
My brain uttered.
How could I love beyond limits?
How could I regard myself as nothing?

Pains that run in my heart
In uncontrollable fashion are made by me.
I have acted against myself.
Given my soul to love without thinking.

Love proved a betrayal.
Took better road for better gains.
It used me I can't say.

To be used, I presented myself.
It simply went when I was useful no more.

Where is my heart?
Where is my soul?
What piece of mine is intact and secured?
None.
I have brought myself to a blocked road.
No trace of lightness.
In my veins, a heavy load.

I have been so cruel towards my existence.
To my dignity ,
I gave little to no importance.
Love came to flow away.
In process I crushed myself.
What do I hold now?

No rush towards death,
I am no coward.
Everyday I am going to burn, burn and burn
To produce enough light

To get back my life.
I am on a new journey,
To re-discover my new self.

UNCONVENTIONAL ME

I don't claim I am different.
I would rather term myself weird.
For I behave like a dumb ,
When I accidentally find myself
In a lavish social setting.
You don't appear like a girl.
Your face needs to see
The world of makeup.
These are usual sentences,
By which a hello to me is followed up.
Basically I am no different.
I qualify well to be called a human.
It's their parameters that point me out,
That intend to classify me unconventional.
I don't claim I am different.
I simply like to say I am weirdly normal.

I AM A LESBIAN

I was born in humble circumstances.
A normal girl, with simple desires,
Sometimes crazy feelings.

My childhood was occupied
In running after balloons,
Reading story books at noon's and
Making noise in my grandmother's room.

Having very few friends,
I mostly enjoyed solitude.
Course took a new turn however,
When I stepped in world's realm.

So vivid, the picture in my mind,
I first saw her sitting in canteen
At the last corner table.
Big glasses surrounding her eyes

And a coffee cup.

Her curly hair was swinging
Over her soft cheeks.
Her smile like a lightning strike.
My heart was losing itself.
I was always nervous around her.

In corridors, on stairs, in meeting halls,
I started liking the office more.
Looking for her was becoming my new job.
"What are these feelings,"
I often asked myself.

It was pretty clear I was in Love.
This girl was falling for a girl.
This girl was going after a girl.
This girl was loving a girl.

For everyone else it was awkward.
For me it was only love;
Neither awkward, nor weird.
It was just love,
I was doing nothing exceptional.

I couldn't complete my story.
She left city unexpectedly.
I couldn't say bye to her.
I couldn't express anything.
A memory.

She was my first love.
She is my first love.
Lesbian or what I don't want to care.
I am blessed for being chosen by love.

FORGIVENESS

My dear self!
You are more knowledgeable,
Part and parcel of Divine,
Source and sink of brilliant lights,
Dwelling of love.
You aren't meant to be closed.
Open up.

Cast off weight of time bygone.
Don't harbour grudges.
Don't condemn yourself.
Black stains on white papers
Can't choke your blood,
Steal your courage.

Night isn't there in sky.
You have dammed the flow.
Stillness will stale you.

Don’t recreate moments already dead.
Guilt don’t accumulate.
Let it loose.

Tears are burdening your eyelids.
End this consistent conviction.
Don’t call yourself a criminal.
Your choices, your ethics, your principles.
Own them. So harshly,
Don’t judge yourself.

Follies shouldn’t lock you away
From knowledge.
Imbibe dark.
For eternal light it then makes way.
Run, walk, crawl,
Don’t stop.

Let forgiveness touch you.
Hug yourself.

Cursing, you don't deserve.
To your own self, don't be so unjust.

You aren't a sinner.
You are made of
Most pure, most pious.
Accept yourself.
Reach to yourself.
Love yourself.

LAPSUS CREATIONS

Who Are We?

Dreams are limitless and so is our vision. Being **India's 1st "Lead by Authors" Publication House**, Lapsus Creations connect your dreams with vision.

With our Guided Publishing approach, authors will have their own dedicated team of experts working alongside for their **BOOK** to come alive. We guide them from the very initial stage of their writing journey till, and after the book is successfully published. While keeping quality at the forefront, we understand the needs of a writer and work towards fulfilling them at zero extra cost.

Promoting creativity across the world is what we are determined about. While we work on the dreams of our authors, we alongside take care of their choices too.

With Lapsus Creations authors have the leverage to choose what they want for their dream book. We firmly believe in, **Of the Authors, By the Authors, For the Authors.**

Every dream has the right to get connected to its vision and Lapsus Creations has taken this initiative. Publishing every dream is our vision and hence we thrive on our motto **DREAM! VISION! LET'S CONNECT?**

www.ingramcontent.com/pod-product-compliance
Lightning Source LLC
Chambersburg PA
CBHW050017170726
48282CB00025B/437
9788194211280